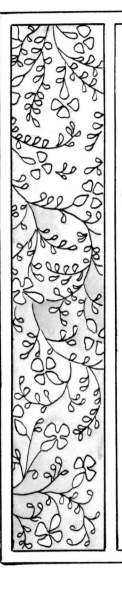

The
Anne of Green Gables
Cookbook

By Kate Macdonald
Illustrated by Barbara Di Lella

OXFORD
UNIVERSITY PRESS

OXFORD

UNIVERSITY PRESS

70 Wynford Drive, Don Mills, Ontario, M3C 1J9
www.oup.com/ca

Oxford University Press is a department of the University of Oxford.
It furthers the University's objective of excellence in research, scholarship,
and education by publishing worldwide in

Oxford New York

Auckland Bangkok Buenos Aires Cape Town Chennai
Dar es Salaam Delhi Hong Kong Istanbul Karachi Kolkata
Kuala Lumpur Madrid Melbourne Mexico City Mumbai
Nairobi São Paulo Shanghai Taipei Tokyo Toronto

FOR MY DAD

NATIONAL LIBRARY OF CANADA CATALOGUING IN PUBLICATION
Macdonald, Kate
The Anne of Green Gables cookbook/by Kate Macdonald;
Illustrated by Barbara DiLella
ISBN 0-19-541919-7

1. Cookery — Juvenile literature.
II. DiLella, Barbara.   III. Title.
TX652.5.M24 2003   j641.5′123   C2003-900052-4
OXFORD is a trademark of Oxford University Press
© Kate Macdonald 2003
1 2 3 4 5 – 07 06 05 04 03
Printed and bound in Hong Kong

Contents

"There, there, never mind your kissing nonsense. I'd sooner see you doing strictly as you're told. As for cooking, I mean to begin giving you lessons in that some of these days. But you're so feather-brained, Anne, I've been waiting to see if you'd sober down a little and learn to be steady before I begin. You've got to keep your wits about you in cooking and not stop in the middle of things to let your thoughts rove over all creation." ANNE OF GREEN GABLES, XIII.

Introduction

Anne eventually became a good cook by following Marilla's advice, and you can too. All the recipes in this cookbook were inspired by passages from the Anne books, and if you read them carefully and follow the directions you'll be able to turn out delicious treats for yourself, your friends, and your family.

Remember what Marilla said, though. Keep your wits about you, and keep these general suggestions in mind before you start:

- Check with the grown-ups in the house to make sure you'll be using the kitchen at a convenient time.
- Some kitchen equipment can be dangerous if used improperly. If you don't know how to use a piece of equipment, ask your parents or someone with experience for help or advice.
- Read the recipe two or three times before you begin—just to make sure you understand what you are supposed to do. If there's anything you don't understand, don't be afraid to ask.
- Start with clean hands—and fingernails!

Now you're ready to begin. It's a good idea to gather all the utensils and ingredients before you start cooking. That way you won't have to stop in the middle to look for things.

There are explanations of cooking terms and some useful cooking hints at the front of this cookbook, and all the recipes are arranged to make cooking easy. There's no secret to being a good cook if you do what the recipe tells you. I know that these recipes work, because they were tried and tested by Carolynn Duckworth, a twelve-year-old Toronto girl. Carolynn and I had fun together in the kitchen, and she gave me some good ideas for making the directions clear to inexperienced young cooks. All the things she made were delicious, so I'm sure that whatever you try will be too.

There are a few safety hints you ought to remember:

- When using vegetable peelers or knives, always cut away from yourself so you won't cut your hands.
- When using saucepans, always turn the handles towards the back of the stove so that nobody will bump into them and knock over the hot contents.
- And always make sure you turn off the stove or oven when you're finished.

Last, but not least, if you want to be welcome in the kitchen, be sure to leave it exactly as you found it. Keep your work surface clean—so you can see what you're doing! Clean up any spills as you go along. And while you're waiting for something to cook, it's a good idea to wash up the dishes you've already used. That way you won't have such a big job to do at the end.

If you keep these suggestions and hints in mind and remember what Marilla said, you'll turn out to be just as good a cook as Anne eventually did. And you'll have lots of fun cooking now, and for years to come.

Happy cooking!

Cooking Tips

FIRST: Gather all the ingredients and equipment.

EGGS: When **adding** eggs to any recipe, first break them into a separate bowl. If any shells fall into the eggs, you can remove them easily—so they won't end up in the recipe!
To **separate** eggs, use two bowls. Crack the egg on the rim of one bowl. Pull the shell apart and hold the yolk in one half of the shell. Let the white dribble into one bowl. Then tip the yolk into the other half of the shell and let the rest of the white dribble into the bowl. Put the yolk in the second bowl.

FROSTING: When frosting a layer cake, always make sure to turn the bottom layer over so that its top side is next to the plate. After you frost the bottom layer, put the top layer on—**right side up**—and frost it. This way you'll have two **flat** sides in the middle of your cake—and you won't find the top layer sliding off!

MEASURE: **Butter** or **shortening**. Press it firmly into a measuring cup or spoon until there are no air pockets, or use the water displacement method (see p. 28, step 3).
Brown sugar. Always pack it very firmly into a dry measuring cup.
Flour or **dry ingredients**. Pile them gently into a dry measuring cup, then level them off with a metal spatula.
Liquid Ingredients. Set the measuring cup on the counter and fill it up to the amount you need. To check your measuring, bend down until your eye is level with the desired amount.

TEST: To test a cake for doneness insert a toothpick into the centre. If it comes out clean, it is done. If cake clings to the toothpick, shut the oven door and test again in 5 minutes.

Cooking Terms

BOIL: Heat a liquid until it bubbles.

CREAM: Beat a mixture of **butter** or **shortening** and **sugar** with an electric mixer until it is smooth and creamy.

CUT IN: Add **butter** or **shortening** to a **flour mixture** and cut it with two knives or a pastry blender until the pieces are the size called for in the recipe.

FLOUR: To flour pans after greasing them, sprinkle a little extra flour into the pans and shake them until the whole surface is covered with flour. Shake out any excess flour.

FOLD: With a rubber spatula cut gently down through the mixture, then along the bottom of the bowl, and then up and over in a circular motion. Turn the bowl and repeat until the mixture is gently blended.

GRATE: Scrape an ingredient against the holes in the grater, to make small pieces or shreds.

GREASE: To grease baking pans, hold a small piece of butter in a bit of paper towel or wax paper and rub the butter all over the inside of the pans.

KNEAD: Put the heels of your hands on the dough. Push the dough down and away from you. Fold the dough in half and push down and away again. Then turn the dough ¼ of a turn each time you push, until every part of the dough is kneaded.

PREHEAT: Turn on the oven to the degree given in the recipe. Let the oven reach this temperature before you bake.

SIFT: To remove lumps, put **dry ingredients** through a sifter, then measure the amount you need.

SIMMER: Cook a mixture just below the boiling point. A few bubbles will form slowly and burst before they come to the top.

STEAM: Cook food on a rack in a covered pot over steaming water.

"*You must be real tired and hungry. I'll do the best I can for you in the way of tea but I warn you not to expect anything but bread and butter and some cowcumbers.*"

ANNE OF AVONLEA, XVIII.

Many years ago cucumbers were called "cowcumbers"—probably because this was the English way of pronouncing the old French word *coucombre*.

Cowcumber Boats

INGREDIENTS

⅓ cup elbow macaroni (75 mL)
1 7-ounce can tuna (198 g)
1 medium carrot
1 medium celery stalk
⅓ cup mayonnaise (75 mL)
2 tablespoons lemon juice (30 mL)
½ teaspoon salt (2 mL)
pinch of pepper
3 medium cucumbers

YOU WILL NEED

measuring cups
some water
pinch of salt
small saucepan
wire strainer
medium mixing bowl
can opener
vegetable peeler
grater
knife for chopping
cutting board
measuring spoons
fork
large spoon

1. Put about 3 cups (750 mL) of water and a pinch of salt into the small saucepan. Bring to a boil. Add the elbow macaroni gradually and boil until tender—about 8 to 10 minutes. Drain the macaroni in the wire strainer and put it in the medium mixing bowl.
2. Open the can of tuna and drain it in the wire strainer. Add the tuna to the macaroni.
3. Wash and peel the carrot and grate it into the bowl. Wash and dry the celery and chop it into tiny pieces on the cutting board. Add it to the macaroni and tuna.
4. Measure the mayonnaise, lemon juice, salt, and pepper. Add to the bowl and stir with the fork.
5. Peel the cucumber with the vegetable peeler and cut off the ends. Cut each cucumber in half, lengthwise. With the spoon scoop out and discard the seeds and any watery flesh.
6. Fill each cucumber boat with tuna mixture.

Makes 6 Cowcumber Boats.

"Oh, Anne, mayn't I help you cook the dinner?" implored Diana. "You know I can make splendid lettuce salad." ANNE OF AVONLEA, XVI.

Splendid Lettuce Salad

INGREDIENTS

½ small head iceberg lettuce

½ small bunch romaine lettuce

12 large spinach leaves

2 small celery stalks

1 small green pepper

½ cucumber

2 small tomatoes

½ cup mushrooms (125 mL)

YOU WILL NEED

a basin *or* a large pot
cold water
knife for chopping
knife for slicing
cutting board
large mixing bowl
some paper towels
salad spinner (optional)
large salad bowl

1. Fill the basin or large pot with very cold water. Separate the leaves of the iceberg and romaine lettuce and swish them around in the water.
2. Tear the stems off the spinach leaves and discard them. Put the leaves into the cold water with the lettuce.
3. Wash the celery, green pepper, cucumber, and tomatoes under cold running water. Dry them with paper towels. Cut them into bite-sized pieces and set them aside in the large mixing bowl.
4. With some paper towels, rub the mushrooms under running water to clean them. Dry them thoroughly. Slice the mushrooms thinly and add them to the rest of the vegetables.
5. Remove the lettuce leaves from the cold water and dry them with paper towels or in a salad spinner. Tear them into bite-sized pieces. Add the lettuce to the other vegetables and toss the salad with your hands—be sure they're clean!
6. Wash the spinach leaves carefully in the cold water, then dry them with paper towels. Don't dry the spinach in the salad spinner because the leaves bruise very easily.
7. Line the salad bowl with the spinach leaves, so that they peek out around the edge. Mound the tossed salad in the middle.
8. Serve in individual bowls with a dollop of Thousand Island dressing.

Thousand Island Dressing

1 egg

½ cup mayonnaise (125 mL)

¼ cup milk (50 mL)

2 tablespoons ketchup (30 mL)

2 tablespoons green hamburger relish (30 mL)

1 tablespoon chopped green pepper (15 mL)

1 tablespoon dehydrated onion flakes (15 mL)

YOU WILL NEED

small saucepan with lid
small mixing bowl
fork
measuring cups
measuring spoons
wooden spoon

1. Place the egg into the small saucepan and cover it with cold water—at least 1 inch (2.5 cm) above the egg. Place the saucepan over high heat and bring it to a boil.

2. Remove the saucepan from the heat and put the lid on. Let the egg stand in the hot water for 25 minutes. Cool the egg under cold running water and peel it.

3. With the fork, mash the hard cooked egg in the small mixing bowl. Measure and add the rest of the ingredients and stir with the wooden spoon.

4. Serve on Splendid Lettuce Salad.

One o'clock came ... but no Priscilla or Mrs Morgan. Anne was in an agony.
Everything was done to a turn and the soup was just what soup should be, but
couldn't be depended on to remain so for any length of time. ANNE OF AVONLEA, XVII.

Thick and Creamy Vegetable Soup

INGREDIENTS

2 small yellow onions
2 large celery stalks
2 tablespoons butter (30 mL)
2 medium carrots
1 large potato *or* 2 small ones
½ cup frozen peas (125 mL)
1 cup canned tomatoes (250 mL) *or* 3 small fresh tomatoes
1 teaspoon salt (5 mL)
a pinch of pepper
1 teaspoon basil leaves (5 mL)
1 tablespoon dried parsley (15 mL)
2 cups chicken broth (500 mL) *or* 2 chicken cubes plus 2 cups boiling water (500 mL)
2½ cups milk (625 mL)
1 sliced green onion

YOU WILL NEED
knife for chopping
cutting board
large saucepan
vegetable peeler
can opener
measuring cups
large mixing bowl
measuring spoons
wooden spoon
soup ladle
electric blender

1. Peel the onion and wash the celery. Chop them into tiny pieces on the cutting board.
2. Put the butter into the large saucepan. Add the chopped onion and celery. Cook over low heat until they are soft—about 5 to 7 minutes.
3. Peel the carrots and potatoes and chop them into small pieces. Measure the peas. Set these vegetables aside.
4. Open the canned tomatoes and measure them into the large mixing bowl. Add the salt, pepper, basil, and parsley. Mash the tomatoes and seasonings a bit with the wooden spoon.

5. When the onions and celery are soft, add the chicken broth to the large saucepan. Add the carrots, potatoes, peas, and tomatoes and mix everything with the wooden spoon.
6. Bring the soup to a boil. Turn the heat down to medium. Boil gently to cook the vegetables —about 15 minutes.
7. Pour the soup into the large mixing bowl, then ladle half of it into the blender and blend on a low speed until very smooth. Pour it back into the saucepan. Blend the other half and pour it into the saucepan. Stir in the milk.
8. Heat over medium heat **but don't let it boil**. Ladle the soup into bowls and sprinkle green onion over the top.
Makes 6 8-ounce (250 mL) servings.

Then the girls tripped out to the kitchen, which was filled with appetizing odors
emanating from the oven, where the chickens were already sizzling splendidly.
ANNE OF AVONLEA, XVII.

Saucy Chicken

INGREDIENTS

2½ pounds chicken pieces (1 kg)
1 small yellow onion
1 garlic clove
1 tablespoon butter (15 mL)
¼ cup ketchup (50 mL)
¼ cup white vinegar (50 mL)
2 tablespoons lemon juice (30 mL)
1 tablespoon Worcestershire sauce (15 mL)
2 tablespoons brown sugar (30 mL)
1 teaspoon salt (5 mL)

YOU WILL NEED

paper towel
8 × 8-inch (20 × 20-cm) baking dish
knife for chopping
cutting board
measuring spoons
measuring cups
small saucepan
wooden spoon
oven mitts
large spoon
tongs

1. Preheat the oven to 375°F (190°C).

2. Wash the chicken pieces under cold running water and pat them dry with paper towel. Pull off any large lumps of fat.

3. Arrange the chicken pieces in the baking dish and bake them for 40 minutes.

4. Meanwhile, peel the onion and the garlic clove and chop them very finely, on the cutting board.

5. Melt the butter in the small saucepan. Add the onion and garlic and cook over low heat until the onion is transparent —about 5 minutes.

6. Stir in all the remaining ingredients. Mix with the wooden spoon.

7. Bring the sauce to a boil, then turn down the heat to low and simmer for 10 minutes.

8. When the chicken has baked for 40 minutes, use the oven mitts to take the baking dish from the oven. Drain off any juice. Spoon half the sauce over the chicken and put it back in the oven for 10 minutes.

9. Remove the chicken from the oven again. With the tongs turn the chicken pieces over. Spoon the rest of the sauce on top and bake for another 10 minutes.

(It's great done on the barbecue too!)

Diana Barry's Favourite Raspberry Cordial

INGREDIENTS

2 packages frozen unsweetened raspberries (600 g)

1¼ cups sugar (300 mL)

4 cups boiling water (1 L)

3 lemons

YOU WILL NEED

large saucepan

measuring cups

wooden spoon

potato masher

wire strainer

1. Put the unthawed raspberries into the saucepan and add the sugar.

2. Cook over medium heat, stirring once in a while, for 20-25 minutes, until all the sugar has dissolved.

3. With the potato masher, mash the raspberries and syrup thoroughly.

4. Pour the mixture through the strainer, making sure you extract all the juice. Discard the pulp.

5. Squeeze 2 of the lemons and strain the juice. Add it to the raspberry juice.

6. Boil 4 cups of water and add it to the raspberry juice.

7. Let the raspberry cordial cool, then chill it in the refrigerator.

8. When the cordial is ready to serve, float a thin slice of lemon in each glass.

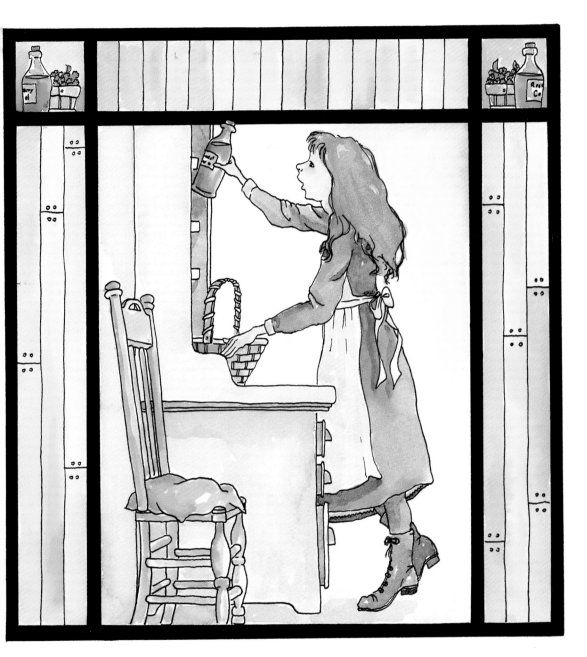

"But it isn't good manners to tell your company what you are going to give them to eat, so I won't tell you what she said we could have to drink. Only it begins with an r and a c and it's a bright red color. I love bright red drinks, don't you? They taste twice as good as any other color." ANNE OF GREEN GABLES, XVI.

The girls sat down by the roots and did full justice to Anne's dainties, even the unpoetical sandwiches being greatly appreciated by hearty, unspoiled appetites sharpened by all the fresh air and exercise they had enjoyed. ANNE OF AVONLEA, XIII.

Poetical Egg Salad Sandwiches

INGREDIENTS

4 eggs

1 celery stalk

3 tablespoons mayonnaise (45 mL)

½ teaspoon salt (2 mL)

a pinch of pepper

¼ cup softened butter (50 mL)

2 tablespoons dried mint *or* dried parsley (30 mL)

8 slices of fresh bread

YOU WILL NEED

small saucepan with lid
cold water
knife for chopping
cutting board
small mixing bowl
fork
measuring spoons
measuring cups
small bowl
large cookie cutter (any shape)
small plastic bag
table knife

1. In the small saucepan cover the eggs with cold water—at least 1 inch (2.5 cm) above the eggs. Place the saucepan over high heat and bring to a boil.
2. Remove the saucepan from the heat and cover it. Let the eggs stand in the hot water for 25 minutes. Uncover the saucepan and put it under cold running water for 10 minutes to cool the eggs.
3. Meanwhile wash the celery stalk under cold running water. Chop it into tiny pieces on the cutting board.
4. Peel the eggs. Add them with the chopped celery to the small mixing bowl and mash them together with the fork.
5. Stir the mayonnaise, salt, and pepper into the egg mixture. Set the egg salad in the refrigerator.
6. Mix the softened butter with the dried mint or parsley in the small bowl. Set it aside.

7. Cut each slice of bread with the large cookie cutter. Save the bread scraps in a little plastic bag for bread crumbs.
8. Butter one side of each bread shape with the minted butter. On half the bread shapes, spread the egg salad. Place the other half of the bread shapes on top. Makes 4 Poetical sandwiches.

Old-fashioned Lemonade

INGREDIENTS

1½ cups sugar (375 mL)

1½ cups water (375 mL)

finely grated peel of 1 lemon

1½ cups lemon juice (375 mL)

ice cubes

cold water

lemon slices

fresh mint leaves (optional)

YOU WILL NEED
large saucepan
grater
measuring cups
measuring spoons
wooden spoon
juicer
1-quart (1 L) jar with a lid
12-ounce (375-mL) glasses

1. Measure the sugar, water, and finely grated lemon peel into the saucepan.

2. While stirring constantly with the wooden spoon, bring the mixture to a boil for 5 minutes. Remove the saucepan from the stove and let the mixture cool.
3. Squeeze 1½ cups (375 mL) lemon juice and add it to the cooled sugar and water mixture.
4. Pour the lemonade syrup into the jar and cover it tightly with the lid. The syrup can be kept in the refrigerator for 2 or 3 weeks.
5. When you're ready to serve the lemonade, put two ice cubes in the bottom of each glass. Pour ¼ cup (50 mL) of lemonade syrup over the ice cubes. Add ¾ cup (200 mL) of cold water and stir.
6. Float a thin slice of lemon and, if you like, a fresh mint leaf on top of each glass.
7. The recipe makes enough syrup for 14 glasses of lemonade.

(For pink lemonade, add ½ cup (125 mL) grenadine syrup to the jar and shake.)

Anne had brought glasses and lemonade for her guests, but for her own part drank cold brook water from a cup fashioned out of birch bark ... Anne thought it more appropriate to the occasion than lemonade. ANNE OF AVONLEA, XIII.

Mrs Rachel and Marilla sat comfortably in the parlor while Anne got the tea and made hot biscuits that were light and white enough to defy even Mrs Rachel's criticism. ANNE OF GREEN GABLES, XXX.

Afternoon Ruby Tea Biscuits

INGREDIENTS

2 cups sifted all-purpose flour (500 mL)

4 teaspoons baking powder (20 mL)

2 tablespoons sugar (30 mL)

½ teaspoon salt (2 mL)

½ cup vegetable shortening (125 mL)

¾ cup milk (200 mL)

½ cup red jam or jelly (125 mL)

YOU WILL NEED

large mixing bowl
sifter
measuring cups
measuring spoons
fork
pastry blender or 2 knives
some extra flour
rolling pin
biscuit cutters (1 large, 1 small)
metal spatula
cookie sheet
oven mitts

1. Preheat the oven to 425°F (220°C).
2. Measure the sifted flour, baking powder, sugar, and salt and mix with the fork in the large mixing bowl.
3. Cut in the vegetable shortening until the mixture looks like coarse bread crumbs.
4. Add the milk and mix it into the flour with the fork—but only until the mixture will form a soft ball.
5. Place the ball of dough on a lightly floured surface and knead it 12 times.
6. Rub some flour onto the rolling pin and roll out the dough until it's about ¼ inch (5 mm) thick.
7. With the large biscuit cutter cut circles, very close together, in the dough. Use a straight downward motion, and don't twist the cutter.
8. With the spatula lift **half** the circles, one at a time, onto the cookie sheet. Arrange them about 1 inch (2.5 cm) apart.

9. With the small cutter cut a hole in the rest of the circles to make rings, and lift out the centres with the spatula. Set these little centres aside.

10. With the spatula place the rings on top of the large circles on the cookie sheet.

11. Put a teaspoonful (5 mL) of jam or jelly in the middle of each ring.

12. Bake the biscuits 12 to 15 minutes, or until puffed and slightly golden. Use oven mitts to take the cookie sheet from the oven.

13. Immediately lift the tea biscuits from the cookie sheet with the metal spatula. Makes 12 ruby tea biscuits.

(With the leftover centres of dough, you could bake some little plain biscuits.)

"I wish I could get Miss Ellen's recipe for pound cake," sighed Aunt Chatty. "She's promised it to me time and again but it never comes. It's an old English family recipe. They're so exclusive about their recipes." ANNE OF WINDY POPLARS, II.

Miss Ellen's Pound Cake

It's called ''Pound Cake'' because all the ingredients used to be added in one-pound quantities. This version is more practical.

INGREDIENTS

1 cup softened butter (250 mL)
1½ cups sugar (375 mL)
6 large eggs
1¾ cups all-purpose flour (450 mL)
½ teaspoon salt (2 mL)
1 teaspoon vanilla (5 mL)

YOU WILL NEED

**5 × 9-inch (12 × 23-cm) loaf pan
measuring cups
large mixing bowl
electric mixer
measuring spoons
wooden spoon
metal spatula
toothpicks
oven mitts
cooling rack
bread knife**

1. Grease and flour the loaf pan. Preheat the oven to 325°F (165°C).

2. With the mixer cream the butter in the mixing bowl until soft, smooth, and fluffy. Add the sugar, a little at a time, beating until light and fluffy.

3. Add the eggs, one at a time. Beat well after adding each egg.

4. With the wooden spoon stir in the flour, salt, and vanilla. Mix well.

5. Spoon the batter into the loaf pan. Smooth the top with the spatula and bake the cake for 1¼ or 1½ hours.

6. Test the cake with a toothpick. If it isn't done, test again in 15 minutes. When the cake is done, use oven mitts to take it from the oven. Let it cool in the pan for 10 minutes.

7. Slide the blade of the metal spatula around the edges of the cake to loosen it from the pan. Turn the cake upside-down on the cooling rack and gently lift off the loaf pan.

8. To serve, cut the pound cake into thin slices with the bread knife.

"No, thank you, Kate, I won't have any more tea ... well, mebbe a macaroon. They don't lie heavy on the stomach, but I'm afraid I've et far too much."
ANNE OF WINDY POPLARS, VIII.

Coconut Macaroons

INGREDIENTS

3 room-temperature eggs

¼ teaspoon cream of tartar (1 mL)

¾ cup icing sugar (200 mL)

1 cup shredded coconut (250 mL)

½ teaspoon almond extract (2 mL)

YOU WILL NEED
scissors

large brown paper bag

cookie sheet

large mixing bowl

small bowl

electric mixer

measuring cups

measuring spoons

rubber spatula

teaspoon

oven mitts

tea towel

1. Preheat the oven to 300°F (150°C).
2. With the scissors, cut the paper bag into a rectangle that will just fit on the cookie sheet.
3. Break the eggs and separate them, putting the yolks in the small bowl and the whites in the large bowl. Beat the whites with the electric mixer until foamy. Add the cream of tartar and beat until the egg whites are stiff and glossy but not dry.
4. With the rubber spatula carefully fold the sugar, coconut, and almond extract into the egg whites. Do not stir.
5. Drop the batter by teaspoonfuls onto the brown-paper-covered cookie sheet —about 1 inch (2.5 cm) apart. Bake the macaroons for 20 or 25 minutes, until they look dry on top.
6. With the oven mitts remove the cookie sheet from the oven. Dampen the tea towel and lay it on the counter. Lift the brown paper and macaroons onto the tea towel. Let them cool completely. Peel the macaroons off the brown paper and put them on a plate.

"You'll put down the old brown tea set. But you can open the little yellow crock of cherry preserves. It's time it was being used anyhow—I believe it's beginning to work. And you can cut some fruit-cake and have some of the cookies and snaps."
ANNE OF GREEN GABLES, XVI.

Maritime Gingersnaps

INGREDIENTS

½ cup molasses (125 mL)

¼ cup shortening (50 mL)

1½ cups all-purpose flour (375 mL)

¼ teaspoon baking powder (1 mL)

2 teaspoons powdered ginger (10 mL)

1 teaspoon cinnamon (5 mL)

1 teaspoon ground cloves (5 mL)

¼ teaspoon salt (1 mL)

YOU WILL NEED

measuring cups
measuring spoons
small saucepan
wooden spoon
large mixing bowl
small drinking glass
2 cookie sheets
oven mitts
cooling rack
metal spatula

1. Place the oven racks in the centre of the oven. Preheat the oven to 375°F (190°C).
2. Measure the molasses and shortening into the small saucepan. With the wooden spoon stir over medium heat until it reaches the boiling point. Immediately remove from the heat.
3. Measure the flour, baking powder, ginger, cinnamon, cloves, and salt into the large mixing bowl. Mix.
4. When the molasses mixture is cool, pour it over the flour mixture. Mix well. Chill the dough in the refrigerator for about 10 minutes.
5. Shape the dough into small balls— about the size of a quarter—and arrange them two inches (5 cm) apart on the cookie sheets.
6. Flatten the balls with the bottom of the small drinking glass—or with your fingers.

7. Bake the gingersnaps until crispy and dry—6 to 8 minutes. Watch them closely—they can burn very easily.

8. When the gingersnaps are done, use oven mitts to take them from the oven. Set them on a cooling rack.

9. Let the gingersnaps cool for 5 minutes, then lift them from the cookie sheet with the metal spatula. Makes about 4 dozen snaps.

The little girls of Avonlea school always pooled their lunches, and to eat three raspberry tarts all alone or even to share them only with one's best chum would have forever and ever branded as "awful mean" the girl who did it. And yet, when the tarts were divided among ten girls you just got enough to tantalize you. ANNE OF GREEN GABLES, XV.

Tantalizing Raspberry Tarts

INGREDIENTS

1 cup all-purpose flour (250 mL)
1 tablespoon sugar (15 mL)
¼ teaspoon salt (1 mL)
6 tablespoons cold butter (90 mL)
1 egg yolk
1 tablespoon water (15 mL)
1 tablespoon lemon juice (15 mL)
1 package frozen unsweetened raspberries, thawed (300 g)
3 tablespoons cornstarch (45 mL)
¼ cup water (50 mL)
¾ cup sugar (200 mL)

YOU WILL NEED

large mixing bowl
measuring cups
measuring spoons
pastry blender *or* 2 knives
2 small bowls
fork
tart tin (12 3-inch [8-cm] tarts)
or muffin tin

small saucepan
wooden spoon
large spoon
oven mitts
cooling rack

1. Preheat the oven to 425°F (220°C).
2. Measure out the flour, sugar, and salt and mix in the large mixing bowl.
3. Fill a liquid measuring cup with 1 cup ·(250 mL) cold water. Remove 6 tablespoons (90 mL) of the water. Push pieces of butter down into the water until the water level reaches 1 cup (250 mL). Pour out the water. Then cut the cold butter into the flour mixture until it looks like tiny peas.
4. Separate the egg into the two small bowls. To the egg yolk, add the tablespoon of water and the lemon juice. Mix with the fork.
5. Sprinkle the egg yolk mixture over the flour mixture. Stir with the fork until the pastry holds together in a ball.

6. With your fingers pull small pieces of pastry from the ball and **press** them evenly against the bottom and sides of each tart tin. The pastry should be about ⅛ inch (3 mm) thick.

7. Refrigerate the tart shells while you make the filling.

8. Put the cornstarch and the water into the small saucepan. Mix with the wooden spoon until smooth. Stir in ¾ cup (200 mL) sugar.

9. Add the thawed raspberries to the small saucepan. Cook over medium-low heat until thick—about 10-15 minutes. Let the mixture cool.

10. Spoon the raspberry filling evenly into each tart shell—they should be no more than ⅔ full.

11. Bake the tarts at 425°F (220°C) for 10 minutes. Then, turn down the oven to 350°F (180°C) and bake them 15 minutes more—or until they are golden brown.

12. Using oven mitts remove the tarts from the oven and set them on a cooling rack. Let them cool for 15 minutes, then gently remove them from the tin.

(Try using 1 cup (250 mL) fresh raspberries, when they're in season. Delicious!)

"Rebecca Dew has been making all my favorite dishes for a week now ... she even devoted ten eggs to angel-cake twice ... and using the 'company china'."
ANNE OF WINDY POPLARS, XIV.

Orange Angel Cake

INGREDIENTS

1 cup all-purpose flour (250 mL)
½ cup icing sugar (125 mL)
½ teaspoon salt (2 mL)
1½ cups room-temperature egg whites (about 10 or 11 eggs) (375 mL)
1 teaspoon vanilla (5 mL)
1 teaspoon orange extract (5 mL)
1 tablespoon finely grated orange peel (15 mL)
1½ teaspoons cream of tartar (7 mL)
1 cup granulated sugar (250 mL)

YOU WILL NEED

sifter
wax paper
measuring cups
measuring spoons
2 medium bowls
large mixing bowl
grater
electric mixer
rubber spatula
large spoon
10-inch (25-cm) tube pan
metal spatula
oven mitts
cooling rack
2 forks

1. Arrange the oven racks so the cake will sit near the bottom. Preheat the oven to 350°F (180°C).

2. Sift the flour onto a piece of wax paper. Measure out 1 cup (250 mL) and put it back into the sifter. Add the icing sugar and salt to the sifter. Sift onto another piece of wax paper. Sift again 4 more times, and set aside.

3. Break the eggs and separate them into the medium bowls. Be sure that no yolk gets into the whites. Set the yolks aside. Measure the egg whites and put them into the large mixing bowl. Add the vanilla, orange extract, and orange peel.

4. Beat the egg whites with the electric mixer until they are foamy. Add the cream of tartar and continue beating until they are firm, but still glossy.

5. Add the granulated sugar, two tablespoons (30 mL) at a time, to the egg whites. Continue beating until they cling to the sides of the bowl and are stiff but not dry.

6. With the rubber spatula, fold in the sifted flour and icing sugar a little at a time. Do not stir.

7. Spoon the batter into the ungreased tube pan. Cut through the batter with the metal spatula to release any large air bubbles, and gently smooth the top. Bake for 45 or 50 minutes.

8. Gently touch the top of the cake. If it springs back, it's done. If your finger leaves a dent, shut the oven door. Check again in 5 minutes.

9. When the cake is done, use oven mitts to remove it from the oven. Turn it upside-down on the cooling rack. Let it cool—about 1 hour.

10. Slide the blade of the metal spatula around the sides and centre of the cake to loosen it. Turn the cake upside down and gently lift off the pan. Ice the cake with orange glaze.

11. When you're ready to serve the cake, don't cut it with a knife. Instead, insert 2 forks, held back to back, where you want to cut and gently tear the cake apart with the forks.

(Save the egg yolks to make extra-rich scrambled eggs.)

Orange Glaze

INGREDIENTS

1¼ cups icing sugar (300 mL)

½ cup orange juice (125 mL)

1 teaspoon vanilla (5 mL)

grated peel of one orange

YOU WILL NEED
measuring cups
measuring spoons
small mixing bowl
wooden spoon
grater
spoon
metal spatula

1. Put the icing sugar and orange juice into the small mixing bowl. Add the vanilla and stir with the wooden spoon.

2. Grate the peel of the orange and add it to the glaze. Stir with the wooden spoon.

3. Spoon the glaze on top of the angel cake. Spread it out to the edges with the metal spatula and let it dribble down the sides.

"Of course I'll stay to tea," said Anne gaily. "I was dying to be asked. My mouth has been watering for some more of your grandma's delicious shortbread ever since I had tea here before." ANNE OF AVONLEA, XIX.

Mrs Irving's Delicious Shortbread

INGREDIENTS

1 cup softened butter (250 mL)
½ cup icing sugar (125 mL)
2 cups all-purpose flour (500 mL)
a pinch of salt
¼ teaspoon baking powder (1 mL)

YOU WILL NEED

**large mixing bowl
electric mixer
measuring cups
measuring spoons
medium mixing bowl
fork
extra flour for dusting
rolling pin
cookie cutters
metal spatula
cookie sheet
extra sugar for sprinkling
oven mitts**

1. Preheat the oven to 350°F (180°C)
2. In the large mixing bowl cream the butter with the electric mixer until it is soft, smooth, and fluffy.
3. Add the icing sugar, a little at a time, and beat until smooth.
4. Measure and add the flour, salt, and baking powder to the medium mixing bowl. Mix with the fork.
5. Add the flour mixture to the butter mixture and stir until well mixed.
6. Dust the rolling pin and a clean place on the counter with the extra flour. Turn the dough onto the floured surface and roll it out into a large circle —about ¼ inch (5 mm) thick.
7. With the cookie cutters cut the dough into any shapes you like.
8. With the metal spatula lift the shortbreads onto an ungreased cookie sheet. Place them about ½ inch (1 cm) apart. Prick each shortbread twice with a fork and sprinkle with sugar.
9. Bake the shortbreads for 20-25 minutes until they turn light brown around the edges.
10. With oven mitts, remove the cookie sheet from the oven. With the metal spatula, immediately lift the shortbreads onto a plate.

"I have never tasted ice cream. Diana tried to explain what it was like, but I guess ice cream is one of those things that are beyond imagination." ANNE OF GREEN GABLES, XIII.

This ice cream is deliciously light and creamy—though it is not as thick as cranked ice cream.

Light and Creamy Vanilla Ice Cream

INGREDIENTS

2 teaspoons gelatin (10 mL)
¼ cup cold water (50 mL)
1 cup milk (250 mL)
½ cup sugar (125 mL)
3 tablespoons corn syrup (45 mL)
1 teaspoon flour (5 mL)
a pinch of salt
1 egg (separated)
2 cups whipping cream (500 mL)
1 tablespoon pure vanilla (15 mL)

YOU WILL NEED

double boiler
measuring spoons
measuring cups
small saucepan
wooden spoon
2 small mixing bowls
fork
wire strainer
electric mixer
2 large mixing bowls
rubber spatula
metal bowl *or* pan

1. Put the whipping cream, electric beaters, and one of the large mixing bowls in the refrigerator to chill.
2. Put about 2 inches (5 cm) of water in the bottom of the double boiler and bring to a boil.
3. Put the gelatin and the cold water in the top pot of the double boiler. Let the gelatin soften for 5 minutes away from the stove.
4. Meanwhile, pour the milk into the small saucepan and place it over medium low heat. When tiny bubbles form around the edge of the pot, the milk is ready.
5. To the gelatin in the top pot of the double boiler add the hot milk, sugar, corn syrup, flour, and salt. Place over the bottom pot containing the boiling water.
6. Stir constantly with the wooden spoon until the mixture thickens —about 15 minutes.
7. Put the lid on and cook the mixture over boiling water for another 10 minutes.

8. Meanwhile, separate the egg into the 2 small mixing bowls. Set aside the egg white for later.

9. Beat the egg yolk **slightly** with a fork. When the 10 minutes are up stir the egg yolk **very slowly** into the mixture on top of the stove. Cook and stir for 1 more minute.

10. Pour the hot ice cream mixture through a wire strainer into the other large mixing bowl.

11. When the ice cream mixture has cooled to room temperature, beat it with the electric mixer until it is light and creamy—about 5 minutes.

12. In the chilled large mixing bowl whip the cold whipping cream with the electric mixer until it falls in large globs and forms a soft peak.

13. Rinse the beaters thoroughly with hot water. Then beat the egg white until it is stiff and glossy but not dry.

14. Very gently with the rubber spatula, fold first the whipped cream, then the egg white into the ice cream mixture. Gently stir in the vanilla.

15. Spoon the mixture into the metal bowl or pan and place in the freezer. Freeze for about 3 or 4 hours—until firm.

"And we had the ice cream. Words fail me to describe that ice cream. Marilla, I assure you it was sublime." ANNE OF GREEN GABLES, XIV.

"I had one chocolate caramel once two years ago and it was simply delicious. I've often dreamed since then that I had a lot of chocolate caramels, but I always wake up just when I'm going to eat them." ANNE OF GREEN GABLES, III.

Chocolate Caramels

INGREDIENTS

1 cup unsalted butter (250 mL)

3 ounces semi-sweet chocolate (84 g)

1¼ cups sweetened condensed milk (300 mL)

4 tablespoons corn syrup (60 mL)

2¼ cups (firmly packed) brown sugar (550 mL)

YOU WILL NEED

8 × 8-inch (20 × 20-cm) baking pan

measuring cups

measuring spoons

large heavy saucepan

wooden spoon

cooling rack

knife

patience

1. Grease the inside of the baking pan.

2. Put the butter, chocolate, sweetened condensed milk, corn syrup, and brown sugar into the large heavy saucepan. Mix with the wooden spoon.

3. Place the saucepan over medium heat and let the mixture come to a boil. Let the chocolate melt completely.

4. Turn the heat down to medium low and cook the mixture for 30 minutes. It should boil gently during this time. With the wooden spoon, stir the mixture constantly the whole time. It's important to stir constantly because candy burns easily.

5. When it's cooked the candy will be very thick. Pour it into the square baking pan and set it on the cooking rack.

6. Let the candy cool completely—about 1½ hours—then cut it into ¾ inch (2 cm) squares.

(This recipe requires lots of patience during the cooking time, but it's well worth it!)

"*Mercy on us, Anne, you've flavored that cake with* anodyne liniment. *I broke the liniment bottle last week and poured what was left into an old empty vanilla bottle. I suppose it's partly my fault—I should have warned you—but for pity's sake, why couldn't you have smelled it?*" ANNE OF GREEN GABLES, XXI.

Here's the cake Anne really meant to make. Be sure you use vanilla—not anodyne liniment!

Anne's Liniment Cake

INGREDIENTS

2 cups sifted all-purpose flour (500 mL)
1 tablespoon baking powder (15 mL)
a pinch of salt
1¼ cups sugar (300 mL)
½ cup melted butter (125 mL)
1 cup milk (250 mL)
3 large eggs
2 teaspoons pure vanilla (10 mL)

YOU WILL NEED

2 9-inch (23-cm) round cake pans
sifter
large mixing bowl
measuring cups
measuring spoons
wooden spoon
electric mixer
small bowl
rubber spatula
toothpicks
2 cooling racks
oven mitts
metal spatula

1. Grease and flour the cake pans. Preheat the oven to 350°F (180°C).
2. Measure out the sifted flour, baking powder, salt, and sugar and mix together in the large bowl.
3. Add the melted butter and the milk to the flour mixture and stir with the wooden spoon.
4. Beat the mixture for 1 minute with the electric mixer.
5. Break the eggs into the small bowl. Add them with the vanilla to the cake batter, then beat with the mixer for another 3 minutes, constantly scraping down the sides of the bowl with the rubber spatula.
6. Pour the cake batter evenly into the two cake pans. Bake for 25 or 30 minutes.
7. Test the cakes with a toothpick. When they are done, use oven mitts to take them from the oven. Let them cool in the pans for 10 minutes.
8. Slide the blade of the metal spatula around the edges of the cakes to loosen them from the pans.

9. Place one of the cakes on a cooling rack. Place a second cooling rack on top. Hold the two racks together and flip the whole thing over. The cake is now upside-down on the rack.

Gently lift off the pan and transfer your cake to a plate. Repeat with the other cake.

10. Let the two layers cool completely before frosting.

Creamy Butter Frosting

INGREDIENTS

¼ cup butter (50 mL)

⅓ cup table cream (75 mL)

1 teaspoon pure vanilla (5 mL)

3 cups icing sugar (750 mL)

YOU WILL NEED

measuring cups

small saucepan

measuring spoons

medium mixing bowl

wooden spoon

electric mixer

metal spatula

1. Melt the butter in the small saucepan over low heat.

2. Put the melted butter, cream, and vanilla into the medium mixing bowl. Mix with the wooden spoon.

3. With the electric mixer, beat in the icing sugar, a little at a time. Continue beating until the frosting is thick and creamy—about 5 minutes.

4. With the metal spatula, spread about ⅓ of the frosting between the two layers. Use the rest to cover the top and the sides of your cake. If you rinse the metal spatula under hot water from time to time while you are frosting the cake, the frosting will be much easier to spread.

(For fun, add 2 or 3 drops—no more—of red food colouring to the frosting to make a pretty pink cake.)

"I just grow cold when I think of my layer cake. Oh, Diana, what if it shouldn't be good! I dreamed last night that I was chased all around by a fearful goblin with a big layer cake for a head." ANNE OF GREEN GABLES, XXI.

Chocolate Goblin's Food Cake

INGREDIENTS

1¾ cups sifted all-purpose flour (450 mL)

1½ teaspoons baking soda (7 mL)

½ teaspoon baking powder (2 mL)

1 teaspoon salt (5 mL)

1½ cups sugar (375 mL)

4 ounces unsweetened chocolate (112 g)

1 cup milk (250 mL)

¾ cup melted butter (200 mL)

3 large eggs

1 teaspoon pure vanilla (5 mL)

YOU WILL NEED

2 9-inch (23-cm) round cake pans
small saucepan
small mixing bowl
sifter
large mixing bowl
measuring cups
measuring spoons
wooden spoon
electric mixer
small bowl
rubber spatula
toothpicks
2 cooling racks
oven mitts
metal spatula

1. Arrange the oven racks so that the cakes will sit in the centre of the oven. Preheat the oven to 350°F (180°C).
2. Grease and flour the cake pans.
3. In the small saucepan boil a little water —about 1 cup (250 mL). Set the small mixing bowl over the boiling water and add the chocolate. Turn the heat to low and melt the chocolate. Remove the small bowl and let it cool.
4. Measure the sifted flour, baking soda, baking powder, salt, and sugar into the large mixing bowl. Mix with the wooden spoon.
5. Add the chocolate, milk, and melted butter to the flour mixture. Mix with the wooden spoon, then beat for 1 minute with the electric mixer.

6. Break the eggs into the small bowl. Add them, with the vanilla, to the cake batter. Beat with the mixer for another 3 minutes, constantly scraping down the sides of the bowl with the rubber spatula.

7. Pour the cake batter evenly into the two cake pans. Bake the cakes for 30 or 35 minutes.

8. Test the cakes with a toothpick. When they are done use oven mitts to take them from the oven. Let them cool in the pans for 10 minutes.

9. Slide the blade of the metal spatula around the edges of the cakes to loosen them from the pans.

10. Place one of the cakes on a cooling rack. Place a second cooling rack on top. Hold the two racks and flip the whole thing over. The cake is now upside-down on the rack. Gently lift off the pan and transfer your cake to a plate. Repeat with the other cake.

11. Let the two layers cool completely before frosting. Frost with Chocolate Fudge Frosting (page 42).

Chocolate Fudge Frosting

INGREDIENTS

2 cups semi-sweet chocolate chips (500 mL)

¼ cup vegetable shortening (50 mL)

3 cups icing sugar (750 mL)

⅓ cup milk (75 mL)

YOU WILL NEED

double boiler
measuring cups
wooden spoon
electric mixer
hot water
metal spatula

1. Put 2 inches (5 cm) of water in the bottom of the double boiler and simmer.

2. Add the chocolate chips and the vegetable shortening to the top pot of the double boiler. Set it over the simmering water and let the chocolate chips and the shortening melt.

3. Stir in the icing sugar, a little at a time, with the wooden spoon. Add the milk. Remove the top pot from the heat.

4. Beat the frosting with the electric mixer until it is thick and creamy —about 5 minutes.

5. With the metal spatula, spread about ⅓ of the frosting between the two layers and use the rest to cover the top and sides of your cake. If you rinse the metal spatula under hot water from time to time while frosting the cake, the frosting will spread more easily.

"I wish people could live on pudding. Why can't they, Marilla? I want to know."
ANNE OF AVONLEA, XXVII.

Creamy Butterscotch Pudding

INGREDIENTS

1 cup (firmly packed) brown sugar (250 mL)

2 tablespoons cornstarch (30 mL)

¼ teaspoon salt (1 mL)

2 cups milk (500 mL)

2 egg yolks

2 tablespoons butter (30 mL)

1 teaspoon vanilla (5 mL)

YOU WILL NEED

2 small mixing bowls
fork
heavy medium saucepan
measuring cups
measuring spoons
wooden spoon
serving bowl
Plastic wrap

1. Break the eggs and separate them into the two small mixing bowls. Beat the yolks with the fork and set them aside.
2. Combine the brown sugar, cornstarch, and salt in the medium saucepan. With the wooden spoon gradually stir in the milk.
3. Place the saucepan over medium heat. Cook and stir the mixture until it is thick and bubbling—about 10-15 minutes. Stir and cook for 2 more minutes, and then take the saucepan off the heat.
4. Dip a measuring cup into the hot mixture and take out about 1 cup (250 mL). Very slowly stir the cup of hot mixture into the egg yolks. Then stir the hot egg-yolk mixture into the large saucepan.
5. Stirring constantly, cook over medium heat for 2 more minutes.
6. Take the saucepan off the heat and add the butter and vanilla. Stir with the wooden spoon until the butter melts.
7. Pour the pudding into the serving bowl. To keep a skin from forming on top, carefully place a piece of plastic wrap over the hot pudding and let it cool—about 1 hour. Remove the plastic wrap and spoon the pudding into small bowls.

"*Everything went right until I saw Marilla coming with the plum pudding in one hand and the pitcher of pudding sauce, warmed up, in the other. Diana, that was a terrible moment. I remembered everything and I just stood up in my place and shrieked out, 'Marilla, you mustn't use that pudding sauce. There was a mouse drowned in it. I forget to tell you before.' Oh, Diana, I shall never forget that awful moment if I live to be a hundred.*" ANNE OF GREEN GABLES, XVI.

Marilla's Plum Pudding

INGREDIENTS

1 cup all purpose-flour (250 mL)
½ cup sugar (125 mL)
½ cup fresh bread crumbs (125 mL)
½ teaspoon baking powder (2 mL)
½ teaspoon salt (2 mL)
½ teaspoon ground cinnamon (2 mL)
½ teaspoon ground nutmeg (2 mL)
½ cup butter (125 mL)
½ cup raisins (125 mL)
½ cup currants (125 mL)
¼ cup chopped walnuts (50 mL)
½ cup milk (125 mL)
¼ cup molasses (50 mL)
1 egg
some boiling water

YOU WILL NEED

1-quart (1-L) bowl *or* pudding mould
extra sugar for sprinkling
knife for chopping
cutting board
extra flour for sprinkling
large mixing bowl
measuring cups
measuring spoons

pastry blender
wooden spoon
small saucepan
small bowl
large pot with lid
aluminum foil
string
canning rack*
toothpicks
oven mitts

*You can use a mason-jar ring OR a hollowed-out tuna-fish can

1. Grease the inside of the pudding mould or bowl, then sprinkle it with a bit of extra sugar. Shake the mould until the inside surface is covered with sugar.
2. Chop the raisins and currants with the knife. Sprinkle them with a little of the extra flour and set them aside.
3. Measure out the flour, sugar, bread crumbs, baking powder, salt, cinnamon, and nutmeg into the large bowl. Mix with the wooden spoon.
4. With the pastry blender, cut in the butter until the mixture looks like coarse bread crumbs.

5. Add the chopped raisins, currants, and walnuts to the flour mixture. Mix with the wooden spoon.

6. Pour ½ cup (125 mL) milk into the small saucepan and place it over low heat. When tiny bubbles form around the edge of the pot, the milk is ready.

7. Break the egg into the small bowl. Then add it to the fruit and flour mixture. Add the hot milk and molasses. With the wooden spoon mix everything well.

8. Spoon the mixture into the pudding mould or bowl. Make a cover for the mould with 2 layers of aluminum foil and butter the side of the foil next to the pudding. Tie string around the foil cover to keep it tight.

9. Set the canning rack in the large pot. Set the covered pudding on top. Carefully pour some boiling water down the side of the large pot until it comes half way up the pudding mould.

10. Set the large pot over high heat until the water boils. Turn the heat down to medium low and put the lid on. (If needed, add more water during the cooking.)

11. Steam the pudding for 3 hours. Insert a clean toothpick into the centre of the pudding (right through the foil). If it comes out clean, the pudding is done. If pudding clings to the toothpick, check again in 15 minutes.

12. When the pudding is done, use oven mitts to remove it from the large pot. Remove the foil and let the pudding stand for 10 minutes.

13. Turn the pudding upside-down onto a warm platter. Serve it with Caramel Pudding Sauce. (Recipe on page 48.)

"Diana, fancy if you can my extreme horror at finding a mouse drowned in that pudding sauce!" ANNE OF GREEN GABLES XVI.

Caramel Pudding Sauce

(without the mouse!)

If you have any pudding sauce left over, don't forget—like Anne did—to cover it tightly.

INGREDIENTS

½ cup firmly packed brown sugar (125 mL)

1½ tablespoons flour (25 mL)

pinch of salt

1 cup boiling water (250 mL)

1 tablespoon butter (15 mL)

½ teaspoon vanilla (2 mL)

YOU WILL NEED

measuring cups
measuring spoons
small saucepan
wooden spoon

1. Combine the brown sugar, flour, and salt in the small saucepan.
2. Very gradually add the boiling water and stir with the wooden spoon.
3. Over low heat stir the mixture until it is thick and creamy—about 5 minutes.
4. When the sauce is thick, remove the saucepan from the heat. Stir in the butter and vanilla. Let the butter melt completely.
5. Serve warm over Marilla's Plum Pudding.